FEA

(IT'

45 FEARLESS SUCCESS TIPS TO PUT INTO ACTION FOR IMMEDIATE RESULTS

DEXTER GODFREY

Fearless Success (It's Up To You): 45 Fearless Success Tips To Put Into Action For Immediate Results

Published by the Fearless Success Team, a Division of Leadership and Sales Academy.

Printed in the United States of America

ISBN: 978-1-939192-01-1

Limits Of Liability/ Disclaimer Of Warranty

The authors and publisher of this book and the accompanying materials have used their best efforts in preparing this program. The authors and publisher make no representation or warranties with respect to the accuracy, applicability, fitness, or completeness of the contents of this program for any purpose.

They disclaim any warranties (expressed or implied), merchantability, or fitness for any particular purpose.

The authors and publisher shall in no event be held liable for any loss or other damages, including but not limited to special, incidental, consequential, or other damages. As always, the advice of a competent legal, tax, accounting or other professional should be sought.

Bulk Book Orders / Version Customization

Most **IChooseFearless.com** titles are available at special quantity discounts for bulk purchases for sales promotions, premiums, fundraising, gifts or educational use.

In other words, if you'd like to purchase a truckload of this book (or even just a dozen or two) to hand out at your company function, an event, or as gifts to your clients, employees or friends we can help you by providing books at a substantial discount over the cover price.

www.IChooseFearless.com

Just contact us at **support@IChooseFearless.com** and we'll send you a quote.

Also, special customized / company specific versions or excerpts can be created to fit your specific needs. So if you'd like to customize this book, please contact us and we'll be happy to discuss your requirements with you.

Our goal is to assist you in getting what you need and also to help our authors to add value to as many people as possible with their books.

For more information, please contact us at I Choose Fearless online at **www.IChooseFearless.com**.

Dedication

To my beautiful and committed wife, Tiffany

and to my "big man" HJ
and my "little man" Chase

I love you all very much and I thank God
every day for bringing you into my life.

Acknowledgements

Mama and Papa Godfrey, you've always believed in and supported me through all my endeavors - thank you from the bottom of my heart.

Mama and Papa Leary - I appreciate your prayers and encouragement.

Melanie, Teddy, and David my business partners and very special people of my inner circle. You will be a part of everything I do.

Jay, thanks for always having my back.

Zuman and the Holden family, Jim, and Terri, you guys knew me before I even knew myself—thanks for traveling this road with me and believing in me when others did not.

Mr. Dan Nice, your example and advice have been priceless. Thank you Matt for your morning prayers and help behind the scenes.

To all my other fellow real estate investors and trainers - thanks for supporting me.

Special thanks to the John Maxwell, Paul Martinelli, Scott Fay and the mentors of the JMT family that helped me to find my voice.

Last but not least, here's to all the people who realize that while we may still have Fear we can choose to be FEARLESS! I did it and you can too!

Dexter

Are you a candidate for Fearless Success?

"You block your dream when you allow your fear to grow bigger than your faith."

~Mary Manin Morrissey

Table Of Contents

Are You Ready?

Today, I encourage you to get ready and set a date:

On this day, ________, I ________________,

(Today's Date) (Your Name)

Will stop allowing fear to hinder me from achieving my God-given purpose.

____

(Signature)

Introduction

Fear is a natural emotion that we all experience at one point or another in life.

With this in mind, I decided to write this book about fear; and not because I've learned the secret to eliminating fear but because it happens to the best of us. The truth is although the title says "Fearless Success," I still encounter fear and so will you.

But I now recognize that the way I handle and face fear boils down to a choice. I can choose to allow fear to rob me of moving forward or I can choose to press through my fear and pursue my God-given destiny. I have chosen the latter and I wrote this book to encourage, inspire, and empower those of you who are ready to do the same.

This book will persuade you to move beyond fear to experience success—if you are willing to conquer the fear that can paralyze you and keep you from greatness.

The tips I share with you in this book are designed to give you that practice and equip you to stay committed.

Being fearless is a mindset, not a state of being. And the phrase "Fearless Success" is all about refusing to let circumstances, people, and other challenges hinder you from reaching your maximum potential. Being fearless also requires continued focus and discipline in reaching your goals.

It is my desire that as you read this book, you will grow and learn because as you know more and you grow more, you'll start to ***fear less***. Then you'll begin to do more and eventually you will have more—ultimately, you will become more!

The choice is yours. Let the fearless success journey begin!

How To Use This Book

As you read each "Tip," consider how you can apply that tip in your daily life. In the page across from the tip, note the question and space for you to write your very own "Fearless Action Step".

Some of the Tips will trigger an "Ah Ha" moment for you—something that clicks and makes you want to remember that thought. Capture it in this book. Use your notes to take action in a way that makes sense to you. Your Fearless Action Step will be unique to you so don't worry about what others have written.

Refer to your notes anytime you are feeling fear and take action. For the best results, we recommend that you review this book along with your notes a minimum of every six months.

"Nothing in life is to be feared,

it is only to be understood.

Now is the time to understand more,

so that we may be fear less."

~ Marie Curie

Chapter 1

Understand Fear

What is fear? For me, it's the lack of confidence and courage that prevents and paralyzes me from fulfilling my God-given potential. Fear is a robber and a thief that can cause major problems if not dealt with purposefully.

When a person allows fear to overtake them, they enable fear to blindfold their confidence and lock it away.

Life's challenges and setbacks can cause us to fear and not walk in the true essence of who we really were created to become.

Question 1:

What are some fears that are controlling your life and preventing you from fulfilling your potential?

Tip #1

Realize That Fear Is A Natural Emotion

As I said before, fear is a natural emotion that we all experience. It is learned through observation or personal experience, and it is typically our inward reaction to some sort of stimuli or perceived threat. Unfortunately, fear can become a manipulating and controlling factor in our lives, often preventing us from living out our potential. On the other hand, fear can be useful in serving as a gauge or warning of possible danger.

Question 2:

What are some of the ways that you "face your fears"?

Tip #2

Realize That Everyone Faces Fear Of Some Sort

Not one person is completely immune from all fear. In fact, we all deal with fear no matter how smart, skilled, wealthy, or experienced we consider ourselves.

However, some people are more determined than others to overcome their fear to pursue their dreams and destiny. The good news is that we can all choose to do just that!

Question 3:

What is the root cause of your fears?

Tip #3

Recognize Your Fear For What It Is...Something You Can Overcome

Whether your fear is a result of impending danger or a lack of self-confidence, I invite you to take time to understand the root cause of your fear and then work from that point to overcome it.

Question 4:

What fears do I ignore and choose not to acknowledge?

Tip #4

Be Honest About Your Fears

It's so easy to act like you aren't afraid of anything. If you don't believe you have any fears, then they don't exist. Right?

Wrong!

Don't ignore your fears—acknowledge them, consider what's causing them, and then work to press past them.

Question 5:

What are my true capabilities?

Tip #5

It Takes Persistence, Commitment And Courage To Overcome Fears

Most of us have a general idea of what we do well, but no clear understanding of our true capabilities. That's because time and time again, we've allowed fear to creep in and cloud the understanding of our abilities.

The good thing about clouds however, is that in time, they eventually clear and the sun (which was there all along) is visible again. The same thing is true of fear. The longer we hang in there and persevere, the more the fear dissolves and confidence takes over.

"Decide whether or not the goal is worth the risk involved. If it is, stop worrying."

~ Amelia Earhart

Chapter 2
Make A Decision
About Fear

Why do we let fear hold us back from fulfilling our purpose in life?

Children are born with an innate boldness; but somewhere along the line that confidence becomes stifled and oppressed by negative people and/or events. As a result, we often feel like giving up on our goals and dreams without fighting for them.

Fear can attack us in so many ways, but you have the choice and power to overcome your fears.

Question 6:

How can I choose to be fearless?

Tip #6

Make A Conscious Decision To Overcome Fear

You can choose the way you deal with fear because how you handle it is your personal choice. In other words—you have the option to be full of fear—that's "fearful" just as much as you have the freedom to reject it and move forward. Make a conscious decision to overcome fear, and by doing this, you'll clear the way to move forward without fear. Every day you can "Choose to be Fearless."

Question 7:

What is my purpose?

Tip #7

Base Your Decisions On Facts Not Fear

Have you ever travelled to a destination for the first time only to realize that you are going in the wrong direction?

The same thing happens when you know what you want, you know what you are good at, and you have a clear vision of your purpose. Yet suddenly just as you are moving on the right track towards your purpose, you allow fear to create a detour in your journey because the voice of fear and its companion doubt usually speak much louder than your voice of reason. "Flip the script" (or change your mind) by turning down the volume on fear and increasing the volume on what you know.

Question 8:

What actions am I not taking because of fear?

What will I gain by taking action?

What opportunities will I miss by not taking action?

Tip #8

Consider The Risk Of Doing It Versus Not Doing It

Always look at the situation two ways before making a decision about "fearing forward" (doing it despite your fear), or not:

(1) Consider what you can gain if you choose to do it.

(2) Consider all the things you are passing up by not trying and missing your opportunity to succeed.

Question 9:

What actions am I not taking?

Tip #9

Take Action And Decide To Be In Control Instead Of Being Controlled By Fear

Fear can cause inaction and paralysis but continuous action will build your confidence.

But whether you take the right steps or not—it's better to step up and take action than to do nothing at all.

Be action focused rather than fear driven. Don't allow your fears to dictate what you do and don't do. Instead, chart your own course and blaze your own trails in life.

Question 10:

Who is holding you back?

Tip #10
Decide Not To Worry About What Others Think

Do you know the reason most people try to prevent others from succeeding? I believe it's because misery loves company. As long as you maintain the status quo and remain complacent, people won't have a problem with you. But as soon as you venture out and experience some level of success, you become a threat to their well-being because your courage towards greatness is a reminder to them of their residence in mediocrity. While it's a hard pill for them to swallow, it's necessary medicine for change.

You were born for greatness, so go ahead and fly like the eagle you were meant to be!

"Inaction breeds doubt and fear. Action breeds confidence and courage. If you want to conquer fear, do not sit home and think about it. Go out and get busy."

~ Dale Carnegie

Chapter 3
Handle Fear Positively And Proactively

So often we tend to handle fear in a negative way. For example, we can revert back to childhood by crying, whining, throwing tantrums, or even playing the blame game. I think we can attribute this to our personal experiences and upbringing. However, at some point we must be willing to take responsibility for our actions. We must examine our fear, grab it by the neck, and take control of it.

Question 11:

What plans can I make to reject fear?

Tip #11

Expect A Visit From Fear, But Don't Accept It

Fear visits us all and frequently brings along its friend—doubt; especially just before we attempt something new.

So plan ahead for fear to come knocking, and when it does—don't open the door.

Question 12:

Who are the people who don't want me to succeed?

How can I avoid those negative people?

Tip #12

Create A Climate Of Safety: Avoid Negative People

As I've journeyed through life I've come to realize one thing about success: Your doubters don't believe you can, and your haters can't stand when you do!

With this in mind, be careful who you choose to share your dreams and plans with, because while you think everyone wants you to succeed, often, it's just the opposite.

PRACTICE

Tip #13

Practice! And When You Think You've Practiced Enough, Practice Some More

Fear is one of life's biggest thieves! Defend yourself against fear by getting prepared. You grow stronger with every step you take to perfect your skill and develop your abilities. You can do this through education, meditation, and activation.

Education: Learn everything about fear and find out how you can overcome it. Education neutralizes fear's power. Also, learn what you can to perfect your strengths.

Question 13:

What steps can I take to practice being fearless?

Meditation: There is power in your words. Say the right words that will help you to overcome your fears. Say the right words aloud to yourself on a continual basis and watch these things manifest in your life.

Activation: Do what you need to do to reach success, even if you have to do it scared…

Question 14:

What steps can I take to move forward in spite of my fear?

Tip #14

Regardless of How You Feel, Keep Moving Forward

Feelings are like a roller coaster; they go up and down. When fear comes knocking at the door of your heart, step away from fear and take time to look at the "big picture" of your situation. When you look at the entire situation, you'll find that fear is only a small part of a very large picture.

Question 15:

What steps can I take to live life to the fullest?

Tip #15

Live Life To The Fullest

As long as you have breath in your body, you have options. You can decide to:

- Use and enjoy your life.
- Make a difference in the lives of others.
- Be remembered for your values, beliefs and contributions.

Make the most of every moment of your life. There's an old anonymous saying that goes something like this: “The past is history, the future is a mystery, and the present is a special gift.” I say forget about your past and don’t frustrate yourself over the future. Instead, unwrap, appreciate and utilize your present. This will be the most blessed "gift" you give to the world.

"Each of us must confront our own fears,

must come face to face with them.

How we handle our fears will determine

where we go with the rest of our lives.

To experience adventure or to be

limited by the fear of it."

~ Judy Blume

Chapter 4

Take Control Of Fear

You have two options: Either you will allow fear to control you or you will take charge of fear.

Since fear is an emotion, make the decision to be the king (or queen) of it. You rule fear and make it bow down to you. Refuse to bow down to fear.

Question 16:

For what new adventure should I plan?

How will I deal with my fear?

Tip #16

Stay Ahead Of Fear, So Fear Doesn't Cause You To Get Left Behind

Don't be caught off guard by fear.

When embarking on something new, plan ahead for how you are going to deal with it. Then just do it!

Question 17:

What are my "bully" fears?

Tip #17

Choose To Face Fear Head On

Think of fear as being a bully that you aren't going to let push you around anymore.

More often than not, when we stand up to a bully, they back off. The same is true for our fears.

Question 18:

What new things do I want to learn?

Tip #18

Go With What You Know, And If You Don't Know Enough—Learn!

If there are things in life you have always wanted to do, but felt you didn't know enough about them, seek ways and people you can learn and grow from.

Always be open to learning new things.

Question 19:

What is my big future plan?

Tip #19

Focus On Writing Your Future Rather Than Reading Your Past

The pen is in your hand. The past is already written, but you hold the pen to write your future.

In fact, your future is nothing more than moments waiting for their opportunity to appear in your life.

Don't be afraid to think big, plan big, and live large.

Question 20:

What role do you plan in this world that adds significance to others?

Tip #20

Know That You Have Value

I've always liked those commercials that offer an assortment of items along with their estimated value, only in the end to show you one last "intangible" item which they refer to as "Priceless."

Well YOU have value too—and that value is "Priceless."

Don't ever sell yourself short or allow fear and doubt to cause you to view your role or existence in this world as insignificant.

"Thinking will not overcome fear

but action will."

~ W. Clement Stone

Chapter 5

Fight Your Fear And Win!

Have you ever watched the end of a boxing match?

Both boxers are exhausted, but in the end (unless it's a draw), one boxer musters up enough strength to fight until he defeats his opponent. Ultimately, he will win and become (or remain) the "Champion.'

You can do the same with fear. Although fear can wear you out, keep fighting until you become the champion over your fear.

Question 21:

What opportunity is hiding behind my fear?

Tip #21

Use Fear To Recognize Opportunity

Fear often comes at the moment a great opportunity arrives in our life. Sometimes, however we miss out on recognizing the opportunity because it has been overshadowed by the feeling of fear.

The next time you are overtaken with fear, begin to search for the opportunity lying within or behind it.

Question 22:

What is the big picture hiding in new opportunities?

Tip #22
Focus On The Opportunity That's Hidden By The Fear

Don't allow fear to rob you of the open doors that life offers you!

The problem comes when we allow our fear to take over and block the opportunities available to us.

Next time that happens to you, recognize it and consciously choose to look at the big picture (the good and bad) instead of just the problem.

Question 23:

What opportunities am I missing by not trying?

Tip #23

Turn The Effects Of Fear Around

Be more afraid of what you will miss out on by not trying, rather than what may or may not happen if you go for it.

I'd much rather try and fail than face a life of wondering what could have been.

Question 24:

What rewards come with a new opportunity?

Tip #24

Be Motivated By Rewards Instead Of Paralysed By Your Fear

The excitement you initially feel when you first discover a new opportunity is the same excitement you need to use to motivate, energize and propel you beyond the fear and doubt you are feeling. Then you can reap the rewards of your efforts.

Question 25:

What can I do to change my outlook and attitude towards new opportunities?

Tip #25

Don't Negotiate With Fear Or Undersell And Devalue Yourself (By Settling For Less)

I have a saying — "Fear is the cheap date when opportunity wants to show you a good time!"

Remember, while it may take longer to change your current situation, in an instant you can change your outlook and attitude towards it.

Tell fear that you deserve to succeed, then know and act like you are worth it!

"We gain strength, and courage, and
confidence by each experience in
which we really stop to look fear
in the face... we must do that
which we think we cannot"

~ Eleanor Roosevelt

Chapter 6
The "Must Have's" When Dealing With Fear

Often when people teach a principle or lesson, they talk about what NOT to do, or what you don't need. But when it comes to overcoming your fear, there are some things you must have. In fact, you can't leave home without them.

Question 26:

What are some ways I can wear "confidence" despite my fear?

Tip #26

Have Confidence In Yourself

I often personify confidence by saying:

"It always seems that when fear and doubt come for a visit, it's when confidence is in the bathroom! And unfortunately from the way it sounds, 'Confidence' is going to be in there for a while!"

Although your confidence may be hiding, you must be willing to get confidence, wear it proudly, and do what you are called to do despite your fear.

Question 27:

What ways can I educate myself in developing confidence?

Tip #27

Have Faith

If fear is cultivated it will become stronger, but if faith in God is cultivated it will achieve mastery.

Feed your faith through proper education and the proper words. Then your fear will starve to death.

Question 28:

What can I delegate if I can't do it myself?

Who can I delegate it to?

Tip #28

Have An "I Can" Attitude

Each one of us has strengths and abilities. The key is to recognize that you can do whatever you need to do.

You should never stop something because of your weaknesses or lack of time.

But if you can't do it, (whether it's due to a lack of skill or time), delegate the task to someone who can do it, as long as it gets done.

Question 29:

What is my vision/purpose?

Tip #29

Have A Vision/Purpose

Roller coasters are fun for the moment, but they aren't a permanent means of transportation. If you want to go somewhere specific, you must plan your trip and means of transportation.

The same is true with your life. Take time to explore your purpose and then map out a plan to get there.

When fear comes, pull out your map and stay on course. Having a written vision helps you avoid fear's detours.

Question 30:

What activities and pursuits make me happy?

Tip #30

Have Fun And Enjoy The Journey

Some people make plans to follow riches while others have their sight on fame. While those aren't bad things to have, don't let money and fame become your only focus and motivation.

If you aren't pursuing something you truly enjoy doing, you will become weary and frustrated along the journey. Then you will quit when times get tough while fear stands there laughing at you because you didn't finish your journey.

Don’t let fear have the last laugh!

"Don't be afraid to go out on a limb.

That's where the fruit is."

~ H. Jackson Browne

Chapter 7
Dexter's
"What Not's" To Fear

While the dictionary describes hundreds of different types of fears, there are some things you cannot fear in order to experience fearless success.

Yes, fear may knock on your front door and try to slip in, but you must allow confidence to rise up and slam the door shut.

Question 31:

What fears of rejection do I have?

Tip #31

Don't Fear Rejection

Fear of rejection can hinder you from establishing and building some of your greatest relationships. Any time you interact with people, there is an opportunity for your feelings to get hurt. But the investment of time and energy in others can also be very rewarding.

Question 32:

What mistakes do I fear?

Tip #32

Don't Fear Making Mistakes Or Taking Risks

Have you ever stopped to think about how babies are persistent in learning how to walk? Even though they fall down many times in the process, they continue to get back up and try it over and over until they eventually master it. In time, they aren't just walking, they are running around.

Don't be afraid to take risks and make mistakes. You may stumble and fall, but if you are persistent in trying again, eventually you will improve and succeed. So embrace the falls and mistakes and use them as "tools" to move forward rather than signs of failure.

Question 33:

What are my gifts?

Tip #33

Don't Fear Showing Your Greatness/Excellence

Marianne Williamson has a wonderful saying that I love. In fact, I like it so much that I taught my oldest son to recite the saying when he was only 4 years old. Here's the beginning of it:

"Our deepest fear is not that we are inadequate. Our deepest fear is that we are powerful beyond measure. It is our light not our darkness that most frightens us..."

Within each of us are valuable gifts that we must share with the world. When we discover, grow and show our gifts and talents to the world—our greatness shines through.

Question 34:

What success do I fear?

Tip #34

Don't Fear Success And Opportunity

It may seem strange to hear me tell you not to fear success, but the truth is, some people fear success. They intentionally avoid doing their best because they are afraid they will do so well that it will cause others to expect more from them.

If you can relate to this, I encourage you to correct that type of thinking, and recognize that it's just another way fear is robbing you of pursuing your dreams.

Question 35:

What fears do I allow to have power?

Tip #35

Don't Fear Fear Itself

Danger and challenging situations will knock on the door of all of our hearts from time to time. Many of us even pray for them to be removed. But the wise person realizes that behind a difficult circumstance he/she can find a lesson, a way to grow, and an opportunity to use the experience as a stepping stone.

While fear is a real emotion, it's only powerful against us when we hand our power over to it. Make a conscious decision not to give fear the ammunition it needs to do its job.

"Death and life are in the power of the tongue..."

~ Proverbs 18:21

Chapter 8
Speaking A Fearless Success Attitude

Recognize that the words you say (especially the words you say to yourself), have the power to escort you to failure or success.

What types of words will you choose?

Take time to consider the following tips by speaking the following words to yourself each day.

Question 36:

What do these words mean to you?

Tip #36

Words Of Wisdom

“I am magnificently and marvelously made for greatness.”

Question 37:

What do these words mean to you?

Tip #37

Words Of Wisdom

"Fear does not reside in me; instead I have power, self-control, self-discipline and love/concern for others."

Question 38:

What do these words mean to you?

Tip #38

Words Of Wisdom

"If it is to be, it is up to me."

Question 39:

What do these words mean to you?

Tip #39

Words Of Wisdom

"I will not allow fear to penetrate my heart and paralyze me."

Question 40:

What do these words mean to you?

Tip #40

Words Of Wisdom

"I am more than a conqueror over every fear I face."

"If you don't like something,

change it.

If you can't change it,

change your attitude."

~ Maya Angelou

Chapter 9
Living Out A Mindset Of Fearless Success

Grammy Award-winning singer, Patti Labelle sang the song "I've Got A New Attitude!"

Take Patti's advice: today is the start of your new life, a new mind, and a new attitude.

You must be willing to lay aside everything that causes you to think negatively or sabotage your success. Now, I can say these words, but you must make the conscious decision to change your mind and your heart so you can become fearless.

Question 41:

What are some ways I can show fearless caring?

To whom can I show fearless caring?

Tip #41

Show The World Your Fearless Caring

Although you will encounter people with varying attitudes throughout your day—some positive, others negative—make a decision to show unconditional care towards all of them.

You may never know how your decision to care for others, including those who aren't particularly kind towards you, could make a major difference in the life of that other person.

Question 42:

What can I do to demonstrate persistence despite my circumstances?

Tip #42

Show The World Your Fearless Marching

As soldiers in life we do not always get a layout of the terrain for our future. I can tell you up ahead that there will be some highs and lows. There will be some happiness and sadness. There will be some surprises and some things you expected.

The good news is that as soldiers we cannot camp out at any one of those emotions. It is the combination of all of them, and the lessons we learn from them as we keep marching, that gives us the victory. Choose to be persistent despite your circumstances.

Question 43:

What are ways I can share my fearless light?

Tip #43

Show The World Your Fearless Light

Today, share yourself with others. Show them your goodness, gifts and talents.

If you see a need, fill it. If you see an opportunity, seize it. Where you see darkness, let your light shine the brightest!

Question 44:

What are ways I can choose fearless growth?

Tip #44

Choose Fearless Growth!

Growth requires change. If you aren't changing, you're not growing.

Today decide to grow by learning something new, going somewhere you've never gone before, meeting someone new, or reading an interesting book you've never read before.

Expose yourself to things that take you out of your comfort zone and away from your norm.

Today - Choose fearless growth!

Question 45:

What are the fear barriers I must break through?

Tip #45

Today And Every Day, Choose Fearless Success!

To fear or not to fear! In other words, is what I want more important than facing the fear that comes with it? If the answer is yes, your breakthrough, growth and prize are on the other side. While fear is a natural emotion, left unattended it feeds off of doubt to grow and rob us of some of life's most precious gifts.

We have a choice. I choose to be Fearless. I hope you will too. Some days I can break through the fear barrier with no problem, and other times it is a little harder. But as long as you and I keep moving forward and fearing less without giving up—we will win!

Fear Quotes

Here are some additional fear quotes to help you.

"I learned that courage was not the absence of fear, but the triumph over it. The brave man is not he who does not feel afraid, but he who conquers that fear."

~Nelson Mandela

"Fear always springs from ignorance."

~Ralph Waldo Emerson

"Don't take counsel of your fears or naysayers."

~Colin Powell

"And one has to understand that braveness is not the absence of fear but rather the strength to keep on going forward despite the fear."

~Paulo Coelho

"When you stop learning, you stop growing."

~John Maxwell

"For God has not given us a spirit of fear, but of power and of love and of a sound mind."

~2 Timothy 1:7

"You can't make decisions based on fear and the possibility of what might happen."

~Michelle Obama

"Faith activates God - Fear activates the Enemy."

~Joel Osteen

"The only thing we have to fear is fear itself."

~Franklin D. Roosevelt

"In order to succeed, your desire for success should be greater than your fear of failure."

~Bill Cosby

About The Author

Award winning speaker Dexter Godfrey is highly sought after by CEO's and companies across the country. An internationally and nationally known speaker, his engaging, yet practical style has earned him invitations as keynote speaker in various business arenas.

Dexter, who is known as "America's Leading Fearless Success" speaker and trainer, is the founder and CEO of the Leadership and Sales Academy, a company specializing in leadership, sales, and personal development training of individuals and organizations. Among his many accomplishments and business ventures, Dexter's most important goal is to add value to people.

He has personally trained and consulted thousands of individuals and sales organizations to achieve over 100 million dollars in sales.

Dexter continues to captivate the hearts of many diverse groups of people as he propels them to reach their maximum potential. He offers his clients entertaining, yet truthful leadership principles that encourage people to overcome their fears and pursue their destiny.

In addition, he is a certified speaker, professional coach, mentor, and founding member of the John Maxwell Team.

Dexter speaks from his heart and connects with his audience. One of Dexter's most requested speeches and workshops, "*Overcoming Fear and Doubt*," demonstrates the importance of dealing with and overcoming major challenges.

Diagnosed with prostate cancer at the early age of 41, Dexter shares with his audience his personal setbacks, the fears, and the battles he faced to come out victoriously through his faith in God.

Whether Dexter speaks to his audiences about overcoming fear and doubt, surviving prostate cancer, or providing customer service, he offers them a fresh, new perspective with practical tips and action steps they can immediately apply to their lives.

If you are seeking an encouraging, engaging speaker who can motivate and inspire others to greatness, Dexter Godfrey is the individual who will provide an unforgettable experience and a personal message that will elevate mindsets, instill hope, and influence your organization.

Contact him today!

Thanks for purchasing this book. If you have been looking for a motivational, business and leadership speaker to blow the top off your next event and really motivate your team, Dexter is the speaker for you.

Dexter travels around the world with his motivational speaking and training; helping people to achieve their goals. He wants to make a difference in everyone's life. He believes that you should leave one of his training sessions inspired and better than you came.

Dexter is one of the most dynamic speakers to work with and you will be glad you hired him!

Visit www.DexterGodfreySpeaks.com and schedule your engagement today!

I've Chosen to Deal with and Overcome My Fear. Will You Join Me?

Visit Us Online

www.IchooseFearless.com

At the **I Choose Fearless** website, you'll find:

- Chapter Excerpts from Selected New Releases
- Original Author and Editor Articles
- Audio Excerpts
- Electronic Newsletters
- Author Contact Information
- Tools and Resources Center
- Plus Much, MUCH More!

Bookmark the **I Choose Fearless** website at:

www.IchooseFearless.com

Looking for a Great Speaker for your next event?

Hire America's Leading Fearless Success Speaker and Certified John Maxwell Trainer Dexter Godfrey.

62566881R00077

Made in the USA
Charleston, SC
18 October 2016